BEACON

the Bright Little Firefly

This book belongs to:

Name ______________________________

Have fun coloring Beacon.

For Jessica and Nikki with love.
—Uncle Joe

This 2014 edition published by Holiday Hill Enterprises, LLC.

ISBN: 978-0-9821203-0-9
1 3 5 7 9 10 8 6 4 2

www.holidayhillfarm.com

The Legend of BEACON the Bright Little Firefly™

Written and created by Joe Troiano

Illustrated by Susan Banta and David Cutting

Did you know fireflies love Independence Day?

It's true.

They do.

But it wasn't always that way.

It all began a long time ago
when a firefly named Beacon chose not to glow.

You see, fireflies had a rule they all had to obey—
every firefly had to glow exactly the same way.

First on…

then off…

then count to ten…

then on…

then off…

then start
over again.

Each firefly going along with the crowd
because glowing your own way just wasn't allowed.

But Beacon marched to a different drum.
He thought flashing your taillight ought to be fun.
He believed every firefly should have the right
to decide when and where to light his or her light.

So one night in the meadow when it was time to glow,
Beacon turned off his light and just said, “No!”
And when every other firefly shut his or her light
Beacon turned his on extra bright.

It got so confusing that before very long
every firefly in the sky was flashing all wrong.

And they all knew who started
the trouble that night.
So Beacon was grounded.
He had to shut off his light.

But Beacon knew he was right.
He knew it through and through.
And before very long
everyone else knew it too.

The Holiday Hill Farm fireworks display takes place in the meadow each Independence Day.

Families and friends gather around and spread bedsheets and blankets all over the ground.

Then they "oooh" and they "aaah"
at the rocket's red glare
and stare up at the colors that burst in the air.

But that night when rain clouds came rolling by
no one could see the fireworks high in the sky.
Farmer Hill told the crowd that for the first time ever
the fireworks would be cancelled because of the weather.

A little girl started crying.
Other children did too.
Beacon thought, "I can cheer them up.
"I know just what to do."

He flew high.

He flew low.

He flew fast.

He … flew … slow.

He flew onto that little girl's nose and started to glow.

Then Beacon flew to the next boy and girl down the row and performed his own little fireworks show.

He started out flashing two DOTS and a DASH.
Then he flickered a little quicker—
DOT DOT DOT   DOT DASH.

Soon every child in every row
was watching Beacon the Bright Little Firefly
put on a show.

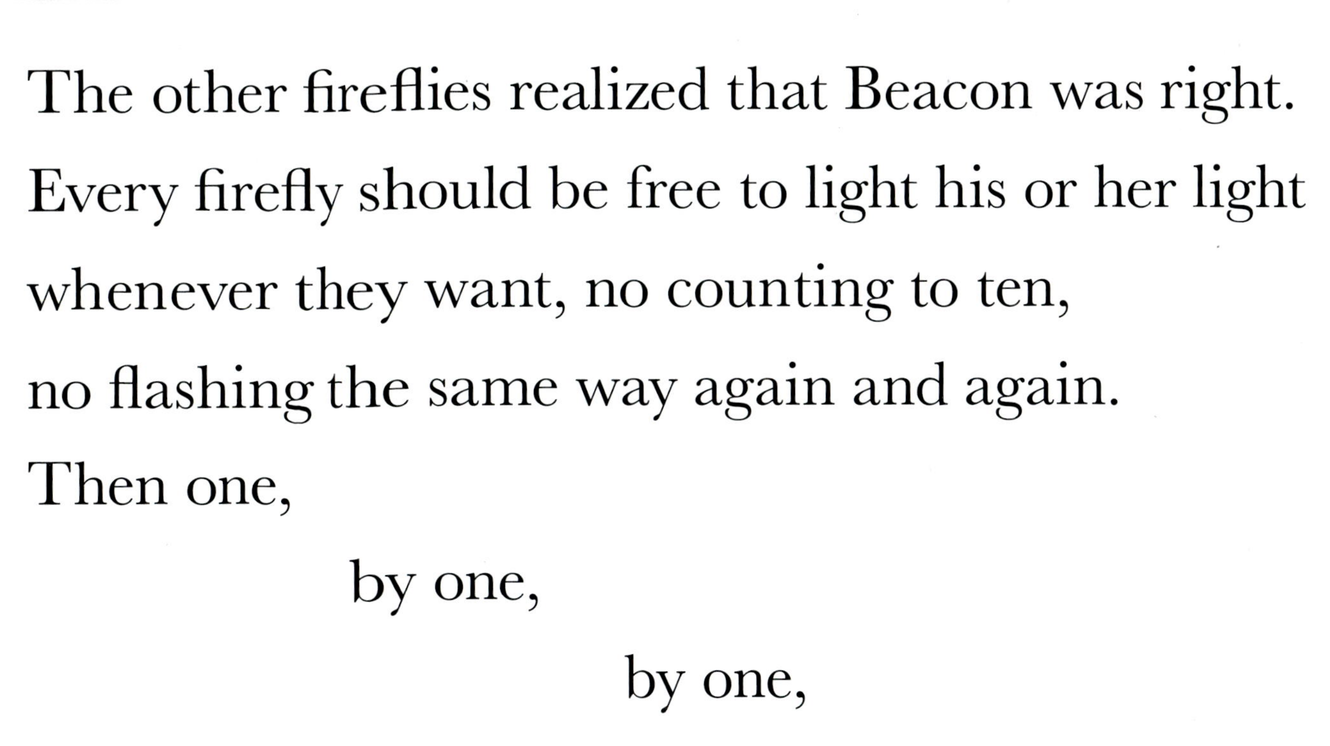

The other fireflies realized that Beacon was right.
Every firefly should be free to light his or her light
whenever they want, no counting to ten,
no flashing the same way again and again.
Then one,
by one,
by one,
by one,
they flew over to Beacon and joined in the fun.

And for the finale
Beacon knew just what to do.
He flew through the raspberries
and the blueberries too.

Then he flew back to the meadow,
covered in goo.
He turned on his taillight—
it flashed red, white and blue!
The children all cheered as Beacon flew by
flashing his taillight high in the sky.

So the next time you see fireworks light up the sky,
imagine that they're Beacon and his friends flying by.

And remember…
freedom to Beacon means be who you are.
You can glow soft and low or you can shine like a star.

But whichever you choose and whatever you do,
the choice that you choose should be chosen by you.

And if you forget, don't get upset.
Look out your window on a hot summer night
and watch how differently
each firefly lights his or her light.

Other HOLiDAY HiLL FARM® Books

EVERY DAY iS A HOLiDAY™

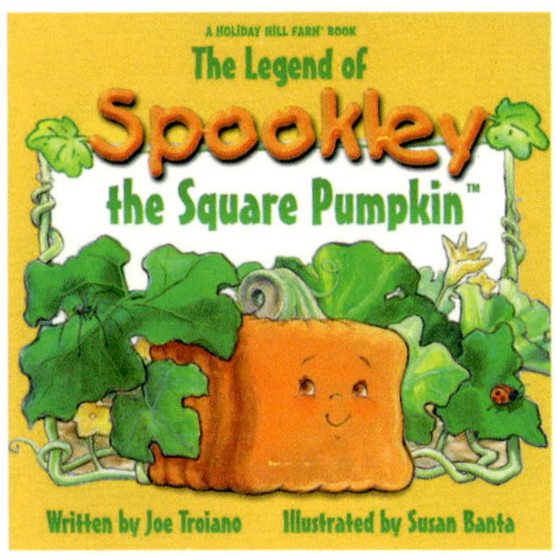

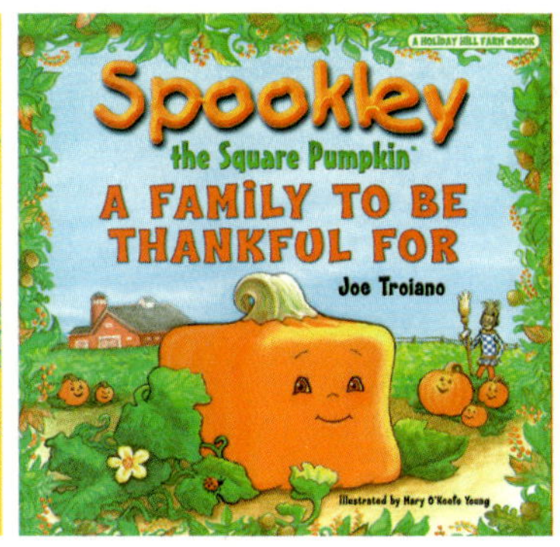

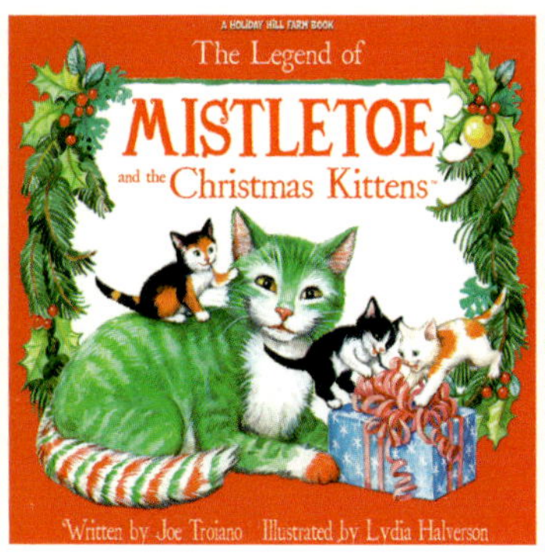

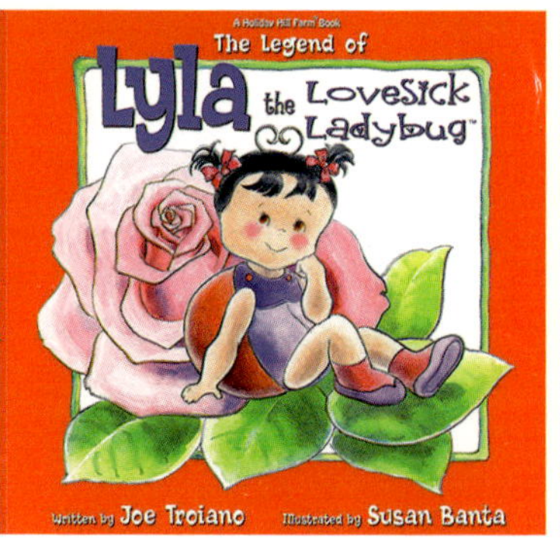

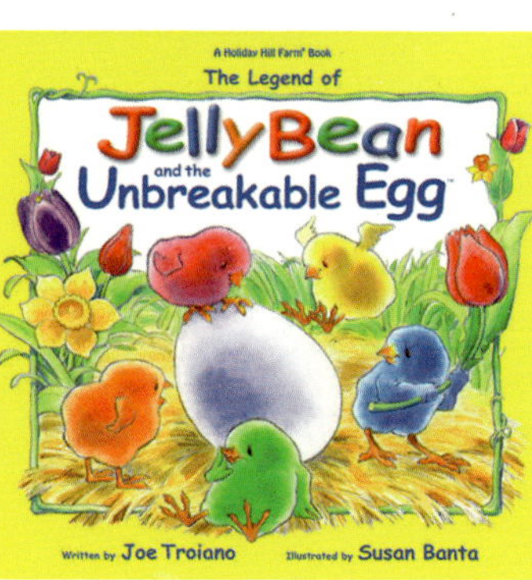

Visit www.holidayhillfarm.com for more Holiday Hill Farm titles.